W9-BZZ-999

David Karp and

Tumblr

INTERNET BIOGRAPHIES™

David Karp and

Tumblr

MONIQUE VESCIA

ROSEN
PUBLISHING®

New York

Published in 2014 by The Rosen Publishing Group, Inc.
29 East 21st Street, New York, NY 10010

First Edition

Library of Congress Cataloging-in-Publication Data

Vescia, Monique.
David Karp and Tumblr/Monique Vescia.—First edition.
    pages cm.—(Internet biographies)
Includes bibliographical references and index.
ISBN 978-1-4488-9528-1 (library binding)
1. Karp, David, 1986—Juvenile literature. 2. Webmasters—United
States—Biography—Juvenile literature. 3. Computer programmers
—United States—Biography—Juvenile literature. 4. Tumblr
(Electronic resource)—Juvenile literature. 5. Blogs—Juvenile
literature. I. Title.
TK5102.56.K37V47 2014
338.7'61006752092—dc23
[B]

2012036728

Manufactured in the United States of America

CPSIA Compliance Information: Batch #S13YA: For further information, contact Rosen Publishing, New York, New
York, at 1-800-237-9932.

Contents

INTRODUCTION

At a Tumblr meetup somewhere in New York City, a hosted gathering where Tumblr users go to connect with one another in person, you might find a crowd of excited twenty-somethings clutching their smartphones and clustering around a tall and skinny young man with dark shaggy hair, intense blue eyes, and a shadow of razor stubble on his chin. David Karp, wearing his usual uniform of a patterned shirt and a gray hoodie, is the founder and CEO of the blogging platform Tumblr, and in the world of social networks he has rock-star status.

David Karp's remarkable transformation from a shy and introverted boy who struggled in school to the poised and articulate leader of a white-hot Internet start-up worth many millions of dollars happened fast, but not overnight. Karp was gifted with intelligence and drive, as well as the willingness to work very hard, but he also had

Blogging tools such as Tumblr (http://www.tumblr.com) have transformed social media networks by allowing users to access, both at home and remotely, a much wider range of content.

the good fortune to find generous mentors who helped guide and advise him along the way.

Early on in his life, Karp deliberately sought out a different path from that of his peers. His mother, Barbara Ackerman, has said that, from the beginning, her eldest son was always very focused and driven. A socially awkward teen, he chose to drop out of a very prestigious high school before his sophomore year and began teaching himself how to program computers. When he was just seventeen, he traveled to Tokyo, Japan, on his own and lived there for five months.

When people started hiring him to write computer code, Karp might have gone on to earn a good living as a computer programmer. However, like other highly creative individuals, Karp often thinks outside the box. It bothered him that the available blogging platforms seemed to be built for writers rather than visual artists. He started thinking about how to design a platform that would be elegant and easy to use and that would allow people to freely express their creativity. As some of the people who know him well have pointed out, Karp seems to have a natural instinct for knowing what will work on the Web. However, in interviews, he insists that he wasn't trying to transform the art of blogging when he came up with the idea for a microblogging service called Tumblr—he just wanted to make something that he could use.

Having been born in the 1980s, David is in the company of other successful young Internet entrepreneurs, such as Facebook founders Mark Zuckerberg and Dustin Moskovitz, as well as Matt Mullenweg, founder of the popular blogging platform WordPress. All of these bright, young innovators came of age in a generation of digital natives. They grew up online, in a manner of speaking, and each would have a big impact on the history of social networks and the new phase of the Internet's evolution, often called Web 2.0.

If you were lucky enough to get close to him at that Tumblr meetup and engage him in conversation, you would find that David Karp is a very upbeat and positive person. He has a good sense of humor and highly values creativity in others. Also, he might tell you that the first decade of the twenty-first century was an especially exciting time to be alive. For someone with big ideas who was willing to work hard and carve out an unconventional path, anything seemed possible.

CHAPTER 1

Meet the Creator of Tumblr

"Mr. Karp is tall and skinny, with unflinching blue eyes and a mop of brown hair. He speaks incredibly fast and in complete paragraphs." That's how David Karp, the creator of Tumblr, describes himself in his tumblelog, or microblog, quoting from a newspaper article written about him. His portrait on his blog, called David's Log, is a large-headed cartoon avatar in a black T-shirt clutching a coffee mug. He probably wouldn't stand out in a crowd in his generic outfit of Converse sneakers, jeans, and a hoodie sweatshirt worn over a patterned shirt. Yet Karp is an extraordinary young man. Like other Internet pioneers such as Facebook's Mark Zuckerberg and Apple's Steve Jobs, Karp made a name for himself when most people his age are happy just goofing around.

David Karp was born in New York City on July 6, 1986, and grew up on Manhattan's Upper West Side. Bordered by Central Park, this vibrant New York City

Native New Yorker and Internet entrepreneur David Karp would soon become known as one of the rock stars of social media.

neighborhood features many distinctive architectural and cultural landmarks. They include Lincoln Center—home of the Metropolitan Opera, New York City Ballet, and the New York Philharmonic Orchestra—as well as the prestigious Julliard School of music and the American Museum of Natural History.

During the 1980s, the Upper West Side saw an explosion of restaurants and cafés along Broadway, Columbus Avenue, and Amsterdam Avenue. Unlike many American cities today, New York City is a place where most people walk or take public transportation. This allows individuals from all walks of life to rub elbows. New York attracts students, lawyers, bankers, artists, actors, ordinary families, and musicians, such as Emmy-winning composer Michael Karp, who also happens to be David's father.

Growing up in such a lively and visually stimulating environment probably helped to make Karp into a creative person. It may have even planted the seeds in his brain for a wonderful idea: how to design a virtual space where people could interact and express their individual creativity and celebrate the creativity of others.

A DIGITAL EDUCATION

Until eighth grade, David attended an Upper West Side private coeducational prep school called the Calhoun School, where his mother, Barbara Ackerman, is a first-grade science teacher. From an early age, David proved that he had a lot more on his mind than did the majority of his peers, including a keen interest in computers.

When David was eleven, he picked up a copy of *HTML for Dummies*. With the help of this book he spent a summer teaching himself computer code. Big software companies such as Oracle and Mercury Computer Systems fascinated him, and he dreamed of one day starting his own software company. He was obsessed with Steve Jobs, who had returned to struggling Apple Computer as CEO in 1997 and sparked the renaissance of the company. In his spare time, David worked at Tekserve, a Macintosh repair specialist, further honing his computer skills. Of his goals during that period of his life, he remarked in an interview with *Wired* magazine, "All I aspired to be was one of the guys that wears a cool anti-static bracelet and gets to take apart computers all day long."

In the late 1990s, when the Internet was dominated by dial-up services such as Compuserve, America Online (AOL), and Prodigy, accessing the Internet at home was still a new thing for most people, and social networks were relatively basic. In interviews, Karp often refers fondly to the days when he and his Calhoun School classmates would come home from school and then reconnect in AOL chat rooms, instant messaging each other (a new feature at that time) and sharing gossip, music, and sometimes even

David Karp sharpened his computer skills while working at the Tekserve store in New York City, which sells and services Macintosh computers.

pictures. He recalls how socially connected he felt during that period in his life. Fitting into the high school social scene would prove to be much more difficult for David, however.

When he was fourteen, David began working as a summer intern at Frederator Studios, a cartoon production company in midtown Manhattan. The studio was run

An Early Mentor

In interviews where he is asked to give advice to aspiring Internet entrepreneurs, David Karp often mentions the important role that mentors have played in his life and his career. "Find mentors early and listen to them," he counsels.

One of Karp's first mentors was Fred Seibert, president of the Frederator cartoon production company, who hired fourteen-year-old David as an intern. Seibert helped Karp get his next gig, as the chief technology officer (CTO) of UrbanBaby, a Web site for hip New York moms. Self-conscious about his youth, Karp tried to dress older and wore a button-down shirt and tie to work, until Seibert told him it just made him look out of place.

Now Karp's "uniform" consists of hooded sweatshirts and jeans. Seibert believed from the beginning that Karp had extraordinary talents, and he proved it when he became one of the first investors in Tumblr.

by Fred Seibert, a former president of Hanna-Barbera Productions and the creator of the popular television series *The Powerpuff Girls*, among other shows. Karp regards Seibert as one of his earliest mentors and credits

No other secondary school in the world boasts as many Nobel Prize winners among its graduates as the Bronx High School of Science, but David Karp opted to drop out.

him with, among other things, helping him to gain confidence in himself. Despite his young intern's shyness and gawkiness, Seibert could sense there was something special about David. Seibert told *Wired* magazine, "He couldn't quite look you in the eye, and he was very quiet.

But he had amazing ideas." The internship with Frederator proved to be a turning point for David. He realized that the most rewarding hours of the day were those he spent working at the studio. He dreaded having to return to school in the fall.

David was clearly a smart kid and likely to thrive in an academically challenging environment. In 2000, he began attending the Bronx High School of Science, considered one of the top schools for science in the United States. Despite being surrounded by other extremely gifted and talented students, David wasn't happy at Bronx Science, a fact that soon became obvious. Even Fred Seibert recognized that his brilliant intern was having a pretty hard time in the world of high school. David was unlike his younger brother, Kevin, who would go on to study literature at the State University of New York (SUNY) at Stony Brook. David felt ill at ease in a new academic environment and had difficulty socializing with his peers. After a rough start, he and his mother agreed he would be better off being homeschooled, and he dropped out of Bronx Science before his sophomore year. Homeschooling tends to be popular in places where

High-Tech Whiz Kids

When he started out, David Karp was self-conscious about his age and tried to hide his lack of maturity from potential clients. But youth is not necessarily a disadvantage in the world of Internet start-ups, where many of the best and the brightest find success as early as their teens and early twenties. Young people tend to be more creative, open minded, and energetic than their older counterparts. They aren't stuck in traditional ways of looking at the world and solving problems. Digital natives, as they are sometimes called, have grown up online, so to speak, and learn early how to navigate the Web and its social networks. These personality traits and abilities provide a distinct advantage in the swiftly evolving world of Internet development, which helps explain why youth often rules in the high-tech world.

Of course, almost everyone's heard of Apple founder Steve Jobs and Facebook founder Mark Zuckerberg. Here are ten more Internet phenoms who made a big splash before their twenty-fifth birthdays:

- Matt Mullenweg, WordPress: Mullenweg founded the most famous blogging platform in the world at age nineteen.
- Ashley Qualls, Whateverlife: Qualls was just fourteen when she founded the wildly popular

site that offers pictures and graphics for customizing online Web sites.

- Catherine and David Cook, MyYearbook.com: These siblings created a site that helps classmates find one another online, which they eventually sold for $100 million. They came up with the idea when they were both in high school and launched it with the help of their older brother, Geoff.
- Angelo Sotira, DeviantArt: Sotira cofounded this online community at age fourteen.
- Blake Ross, Firefox: Ross cocreated the popular Web browser at age nineteen.
- Dustin Moskovitz, Facebook: Moskovitz cofounded the social network with Mark Zuckerberg, Eduardo Saverin, and Chris Hughes.
- Juliette Brindak, MissOandFriends.com: Brindak founded the online community for tween and teen girls when she was sixteen.
- Noah Everett, TwitPic: When he was twenty-four, Everett founded the service that allows people to easily post pictures to Twitter.
- Pete Cashmore, *Mashable*: Cashmore founded the popular Internet news blog *Mashable* when he was twenty.

schools do not adequately serve the local community. The Upper West Side of Manhattan is not one of those places. Leaving high school was the right decision for David, however. It gave him the chance to concentrate on what most fascinated him and allowed his true talents to blossom.

EARNING A LIVING ONLINE

David's developing reputation as a skilled programmer began to attract clients, who contracted with him to do freelance work. David was still just fifteen when a Web site developer named John Maloney hired him over the phone to write code for a new site. UrbanBaby was aimed at new and expecting mothers. Maloney gave David a project that he thought would take him a few days to complete. When David finished it in just four hours, Maloney recognized that his new employee was an exceptionally talented young man. What he didn't know was that David was just a teenager, since the two had yet to meet in person. UrbanBaby caught on with its intended audience of hip New York moms. Soon David was singlehandedly running the technical side of the business out of his mother's Upper West Side apartment.

David's three years of hard work at UrbanBaby paid off. For the first time in his life, he was making some money. One of the first things he did with his savings was plan a trip to Japan. His mom was surprised. David was only seventeen. Yet, he had already taken some Japanese lessons, made all the arrangements, and purchased his ticket. David ended up staying in Tokyo for five months. "I was holed up in the middle of this world where it was just me on the Internet," he explained to the *Guardian*.

During his stay in Japan, David was trying to drum up more consulting jobs. The problem was that he was still a kid—and he sounded like one. Who would want to hire him? When he spoke to potential clients over the phone, David faked a deep voice to fool them into thinking he was much older than he was—anything to avoid having to meet with a client face-to-face.

Previously, David had set up his own Web consulting firm, "an invention company," which he named David-ville. When he returned from Tokyo with a handful of contracts, David posted an ad on Craigslist in search of another engineer. A young programmer named Marco Arment responded to David's ad, and because David was too nervous to interview Marco on his own, he asked Fred Seibert to sit in. When Marco was first hired, he wasn't entirely sure which of the two was his boss.

In May 2006, UrbanBaby was acquired by CNET Networks. David was surprised to learn that John Maloney had put some shares of the company in David's name. With what he earned from the sale of the parenting site, David rented space from Seibert in the Frederator cartoon studios to house Davidville. He and Arment soon gained a reputation for being skilled coders, but they often annoyed clients when they didn't respond to e-mails on time. Some of the successful projects David and Marco developed for Davidville included a file-sharing site called Senduit, and WorldwideFido, a version of YouTube for dogs.

At one point they found themselves with a two-week gap between projects. That little space of free time provided the opportunity for everything that was to follow. That's when the two went to work on a little side project of David's, an idea he'd been tossing around in his head for a while. It was a microblogging service that would eventually be called Tumblr.

CHAPTER 2

A Better Blogging Platform

The word "blog," coined in 1999, is a mashup of the term "web log." Originally a noun, the term has since evolved into common use as a verb as well, as in "to blog." The earliest blogs were essentially online diaries, where a blogger would record the details of his or her daily experience. Unlike an old-fashioned paper diary, blog entries usually appear in reverse chronological order, with the most current post appearing first, at the top of the screen. Older blog posts are archived, or stored, for future use. And unlike traditional journals or diaries, which people tend to keep for their own private use, blogs are more often public documents, immediately accessible to any reader online, who can (if the blogger wishes) comment on or reply to the entry and provide instant feedback about what's been written.

The first blogs were manually updated sections of existing Web sites. The first bloggers had to know enough

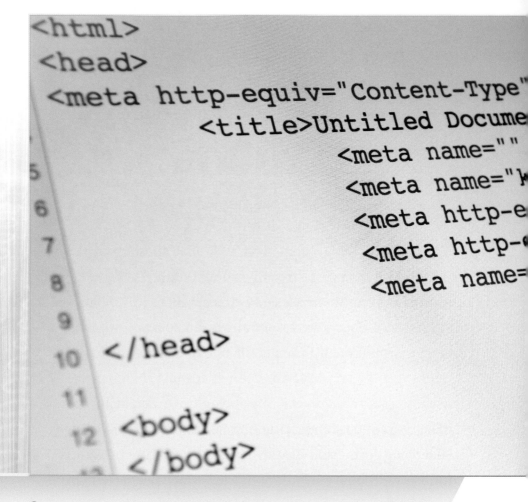

```html
<html>
<head>
<meta http-equiv="Content-Type"
            <title>Untitled Docume
                    <meta name=""
                    <meta name="k
                    <meta http-e
                    <meta http-
                    <meta name=
</head>

<body>
</body>
```

Computer programmers use programming languages or codes such as HTML to direct computers to perform various functions.

HTML (hypertext markup language) computer code to cobble together their own blogs, rather than having a host service do it for them. Early in its evolution, blogging was often dismissed as a forum for rambling, self-indulgent rants. Eventually, bloggers could post short videos of themselves in video blogs, or vlogs, but the main content was written text, since blogs are essentially a form of personal online publishing. As Internet fads go, blogging had a fairly slow development. At the beginning of 1999, there were just twenty-three blogs known to be in existence; by February 2011, that number had climbed to over 156 million, but it took more than a decade to get there. Today, so many blogs exist that they are collectively referred to as the blogosphere.

Blogging became more widespread with the development of hosted blog tools, such as Open Diary (launched 1998), which for the first time allowed readers to comment on a writer's blog entry. All the build-your-own-blog tools developed during this time were free to the user. You could create as many different blogs as you liked on these sites without paying a penny for the privilege. Other typical features of the first hosted blogging platforms included the choice of different blogging templates, or themes, that let you customize the appearance of your blog. Hosted blogging software makes it very easy for anyone to create a Web site of his or her own, which is one reason blogs have become so popular.

In the first wave of hosted blogging platforms, one of the most well known became a host called Blogger. Launched in 1999 at Pyra Labs, Blogger was eventually

One of the first hosted blogging platforms, Blogger (http://www.blogger.com) was created by three friends working at a tiny San Francisco company called Pyra Labs.

purchased by Internet giant Google in 2003. In addition to Blogger, a very popular blogging platform is WordPress, which was first released for download in May 2003. Early weblogs were all about making connections to other Web sites, serving up a mixture of links, as well as commentary and personal thoughts. In December 2004, Merriam-Webster's dictionary proclaimed "blog" the Word of the Year.

Early bloggers often filtered both mainstream and alternative news sources. They found and shared news items that were underreported or ignored by the big media services, arranging these materials in compelling ways. Because of this practice, blogging was initially regarded by some as a subversive activity. Bloggers were also dismissed as reputable sources of information because they used other people's content, sometimes without attribution. Over time, politicians, news organizations, and companies came to recognize the potential of blogs as a means of spreading information and shaping public opinion. Popular bloggers have significant influence within the online community. Today, certain blogs, such as the *Huffington Post*, which covers current events, and *Mashable*, which reports on technology, have become an established part of the mainstream media.

THE MICROBLOG

The available blogging platforms were great for writers who wanted to share lots of editorial content. However, it

Silicon Valley vs. Silicon Alley

"Silicon Valley" is a term used since 1971 to describe the area that extends along the peninsula southwest of San Francisco, California. It refers to the microchips made of silicon first developed and manufactured at electronics firms such as Intel and Hewlett Packard. These microchips held the integrated circuits packed into the guts of most PCs. Thanks to the proximity of Stanford University, which fueled entrepreneurship and innovation in the region, Silicon Valley became the home of high-tech industry giants like Apple, Google, eBay, Yahoo!, and Oracle. Internet start-ups that originate on the East Coast, like Facebook, often pull up stakes and head west. Founded in Boston, when CEO Mark Zuckerberg attended Harvard University, Facebook moved west to Palo Alto, California, just as the social networking site became poised for success. Facebook is currently headquartered in Menlo Park, a city adjacent to Palo Alto.

But it may be a sign of things to come that Facebook opened its first engineering office in New York in 2012, and eBay is also expanding its offices to the Big Apple. David Karp, a native New Yorker, is a big booster for his hometown. New York City is way "cooler than Palo Alto," Karp says. The fact

The Flatiron District, home to Tumblr headquarters, is known as Silicon Alley, New York City's high-tech hub.

that New York is, in Karp's opinion, "the heart of the creative world" has helped his company lure some top talent away from big tech companies. Half of the Tumblr team are "relos," or individuals that have relocated to New York from other places.

Historically, New York is best known as a hub for global media and finance. Fledgling developments in the New York high-tech industry, soon dubbed Silicon Alley, were squelched in the late 1990s, when the dot-com bubble burst and many Internet companies went out of business.

Recently signs point to a New York dot-com reboot, however. People often refer to the so-called second generation of the Internet as "Web 2.0." The term has come to describe a new phase in the evolution of the Internet focused on finding ways for people to collaborate and share information online. The user-driven Web has fueled the development of new media and Internet companies in Manhattan and attracted the venture capitalists that invest in Internet start-ups.

wasn't easy to share other types of material, such as music, photographs, video, and audio. David Karp, who doesn't enjoy writing, felt frustrated by these limitations. When he sat down in front of his computer to create a post on Blogger or WordPress, he felt intimidated by the big block of empty white space staring back at him. When Facebook became popular, this social networking Web site became the go-to place where people went to create a personal profile and connect with other friends online. However, the standard Facebook profile didn't allow users to be very creative or customize the look of their page.

Like Tumblr, WordPress (http://www.wordpress.com) is a free blogging platform that hosts many millions of blogs. Many users maintain blogs on more than one service.

There was, however, something called a microblog, a short-form blogging platform that appealed to Karp. In March 2005, a seventeen-year-old German high school student named Christian Neukirchen had launched what would become the first tumblelog. His first post was, as he described it, "experimental, impressionistic sub-paragraph tumblin'..." The only rule guiding the tumblelog was that the editorial content had to be less than a paragraph. Over the years, Neukirchen's site published

Birth of the Blogosphere

In January 1994, a nineteen-year-old Swarthmore College student named Justin Hall began writing an online diary about his life. Hall was an artistic guy, known for his crazy hairstyles and unconventional behavior. It seemed that no detail of his life was too private or too embarrassing to be included in the diary, which he called Justin's Notes from the Underground. In his rambling entries, Hall wrote about all aspects of his life. He bared it all.

Hall's online postings attracted thousands of followers who were fascinated by the spectacle of apparently uncensored exposure of one person's experience. Many people consider Justin Hall the first blogger.

a unique mishmash of quotes, lyrics, links to other sites, thoughts, and pictures. It provided the prototype for the short-form blog, or microblog, that Tumblr would eventually popularize.

THE LAUNCH OF TUMBLR

At the end of 2006, David Karp and Marco Arment, the two employees of Karp's consulting company, Davidville, had a two-week break between projects. According to *Wired*, Karp had been toying with an idea for a microblog. The first microbloggers, like Christian Neukirchen, had to hack together their own sites from the existing software, which is exactly what Karp and Arment set out to do. They coded a crude version of Tumblr (or "Tumblehub," as it was called during the first six months of its development) and had a private beta version ready by October 2006. They launched the site as a free tumblelogging platform on February 19, 2007.

Karp insists that he didn't set out to create a massively popular microblogging platform. He was just trying to create a tool that better suited his own particular interests and abilities. "I didn't expect anyone to use it," Karp said in the course of an interview at the Internet Week New York festival in May 2012. "It wasn't intended to be viral or popular. It was just intended to be useful."

Apparently plenty of other people found it useful, too: within the first two weeks that this early version of Tumblr was up and running, seventy-five thousand people used it to create blogs. Karp thinks what first appealed to people was how easy it was to customize the code and make it your own. In a March 2012 interview with *Wired*, Karp said, "It was just a big chunk of code you could rip apart and make original. And it attracted this spectacular community of designers and hackers. Over the next few weeks, they built gorgeous things on Tumblr that didn't look like anything else on the Internet."

The social network aspect of Tumblr wasn't part of Karp's original design but rather something that evolved naturally over time and is part of a phenomenon that is now called social blogging. People who were blogging on Tumblr started seeking out one another and making connections. As Karp and Arment saw what was happening, they added features to the service to make it easier for people to find other Tumblr members with shared interests. Karp added directories, which grouped blogs based on the tags that people assigned themselves. Karp and Arment also created a section on the site called Tumblr Radar, where they highlighted interesting blogs that they found on Tumblr.

Great ideas often have a life of their own—especially on the Web, where information travels at light speed. What Tumblr would actually become—a wildly popular social blogging network—seems like an unplanned but successful collaboration between Karp, Arment, and the wider Internet community. As Karp would be the first to acknowledge, the evolution of his original vision for Tumblr had as much to do with how the platform was embraced and utilized by its members as it did with his initial concept of what he wanted to create.

Chapter 3

Tumblr Takes Off

The first one hundred Tumblr users were friends and family of Karp and Arment. However, the service quickly caught on with other creative people. They responded positively to the elegance and flexibility of Karp's design. Soon the blogging platform had become so popular that Davidville's other clients began to feel neglected and annoyed because working on Tumblr was occupying so much of Karp and Arment's time. It wasn't long before Davidville had to stop accepting new work in order to focus exclusively on the Tumblr site. In the day-to-day operations of Tumblr, Karp was responsible for the front-end code and design of the site, also called the user interface. These are the commands that enable users to do what they want on a service. Arment's job was to write the majority of Tumblr's back-end code (the commands that communicate with the server), design the software architecture, and administer the site.

Tumblr uses an interface system called WYSIWYG (What You See Is What You Get), which shows you the effect of the edits you make in a blog post as soon as you make them. Bloggers on Tumblr can easily post all kinds of materials, from words and images to video, audio, and links. While Facebook requires that its members use their actual names, no such demand exists on Tumblr. From the start, Karp's goal for Tumblr was to give its users total freedom of expression. This included being able to make up a new name and identity, if they liked, and to customize the appearance of their blog so that it didn't resemble anyone else's.

FUNDING

A service like Tumblr is free to use but costly to run. So, what keeps the business afloat? Who pays for the rental of office space, furnishings, and equipment? Who shells out the money for the salaries of the engineers, coders, systems director, and company president? Internet start-ups need investors to fund them until they can begin generating their own revenue. People who start their own businesses often approach investors in an effort to raise enough money to get their enterprises off the ground. Like the earliest Tumblr users, some of the first so-called angel investors, or initial investors who help finance a company in its developmental stages, were David Karp's friends and

Sporting his own take on business casual attire, David Karp, CEO of Tumblr, poses confidently in the offices of the company he founded at age twenty-one.

family. Michael Karp, David's dad, invested money in the project. Karp's mentor Fred Seibert believed that his protégé's latest project looked promising, and he also agreed to provide a portion of the necessary funding to get Tumblr up and running.

Investors for Internet companies are often venture capitalists, or VCs, representatives of financial funds who scout out opportunities for profit. If they find a young business that looks like it has the potential for growth, they may invest money in the hope that they will eventually earn a profit on their initial investment.

Start-up businesses, and their investors, may make money when the company either goes public, which means it sells its shares on the stock exchange, or if the business is acquired by another company. Most successful dot-com start-ups rely on venture capital investments. This money typically comes with strings attached: investors often acquire a substantial share of a company's stock, and they may have a say in certain key decisions that the company makes.

By December 2010, Tumblr had raised $30 million in investments from the VC firms Sequoia Capital, Spark Capital, and Union Square Ventures. By September 2011, the company succeeded in raising an additional $85

Reblog

One of Tumblr's most important features, which some analysts consider a key factor in the micro-blogging platform's explosive growth, is the reblog button. Added about six months after Tumblr launched, and symbolized by a square red icon with blue arrows pointing in opposite directions, the reblog button appears beside any content that a person posts on Tumblr. When another member of Tumblr presses "reblog," it transfers the contents of that post to his or her own blog. Reblogging is similar to the retweet function on Twitter (it actually predates it by two years), except that on Tumblr you can see the entire reblogging history of a post, including whoever first posted the content. A popular Tumblr user can display her or his reblog list to show off how many people have reblogged a particular post. Reblogging eventually creates communities of users who share similar interests. In large part because of this feature, Tumblr has become somewhat of a hybrid between a social networking site and a more conventional blogging platform.

Business tycoon Sir Richard Branson has invested in everything from airlines and commercial spaceflight to Internet start-ups such as Tumblr.

million from a group of investors that included British billionaire Richard Branson, founder of the Virgin Group.

When Tumblr's popularity took off, David Karp woke up to find that he had suddenly become a celebrity. Lots of people were drawn to the lanky, twenty-something wonder boy with the piercing eyes, and Karp made the most of it. Every tech journalist was scrambling to schedule an interview with him. Newspapers and magazines, both online and off, wrote articles about him and took his photograph. *Details* magazine named him one of "the Playboys of Tech." He even modeled a sweater for the Japanese fashion brand Uniqlo. During this time, Karp had a very busy social life.

There was at least one temptation that Karp resisted, however: he repeatedly turned down offers to move Tumblr to Silicon Valley. He was convinced that neither he nor his fledgling company would thrive in the hypercompetitive environment of the West Coast. Karp believed that Tumblr's location in the midst of New York City's creative scene, and its connection to the city's many artistic communities, was one essential key to the site's success.

GROWING PAINS

Tumblr's investors smelled a hot property. By July 2010, the site was attracting twenty-five thousand new users each day. Soon, Tumblr's surging popularity began to compromise its ability to handle the volume of new members. Investors urged Karp to hire additional engineers to keep pace with the company's

CEO David Karp in the Tumblr offices alongside the company's "media evangelist" Mark Coatney *(center)* and John Maloney *(right)*, who served as president from 2008 to 2012.

explosive growth, but Karp was confident that his team, which at the time consisted of just two engineers, could handle the increased traffic to the site. On December 5, 2010, just days after the ink was dry on a contract that awarded Tumblr $20 million from Sequoia Capital, the system overloaded and the site crashed. As Karp described it when he was interviewed by *Business Insider* magazine in May 2011, "It was a cascading failure. The wrong server in the wrong place failed, and it took out a whole cluster of servers with it." Tumblr president John Maloney called it "the day Tumblr broke the Internet."

Suddenly, sixteen million blogs were offline. Some users were furious and later posted scathing comments ("Why Tumblr Sucks") about Tumblr on their blogs. The failure inspired the creation of Web sites such as IsTumblrDown and WellBeBackShortly. During the blackout, many frustrated Tumblr users communicated via Twitter.

In the aftermath of the catastrophe, Tumblr's overtaxed lead engineer, Matt Hackett, and systems director Andrew Terng worked forty hours straight (with plenty of caffeine to keep them going) to bring the site back online. While they coded frantically, Karp and his team went on Twitter to tweet the latest developments to concerned users, reassuring them that their tumblelogs would be back up ASAP. Service in some countries was restored within sixteen hours, but getting all of the Tumbler blogs in the United States back online took longer. Once Tumblr was finally up and running again, an apologetic Karp posted an explanation of what had happened and told the world, "We really messed up."

Karp learned a lot from the experience and believes it has made him a better manager. Important lessons that he has taken to heart include not being afraid to assume responsibility for your mistakes and acting quickly to correct the problem. He learned the importance of communicating clearly to one's team and one's investors. Finally, Karp learned not to let his own stubborn perfectionism prevent him from doing what's necessary. Many of his investors had warned him that he needed to hire more engineers, but he had mistakenly believed that he had everything under control.

Other issues Tumblr has struggled with including the prevalence of microblog spam and pornographic content. Web communications services such as Facebook, Word-Press, and Blogger all spend a lot of money fighting junk blogs. Many young Tumblr users aren't savvy enough to separate the spam from the substance and may be lured to disreputable sites, such as fad weight loss and moneymaking schemes, by misleading comments.

THE YEAR OF TUMBLR

Despite the frustration of its users when their blogs went offline, Tumblr's traffic actually increased after the crash and continued on a sharp upswing. The year 2011 turned out to be an amazing time for the company, which more

Hockey Stick Growth

You don't have to be a Canucks fan to know what a hockey stick looks like. When a new Internet company or service begins growing modestly and then suddenly takes off, its growth pattern on a graph resembles a hockey stick, which is where the expression "hockey stick growth" comes from.

While every Internet start-up wants its business to be massively successful, managing this kind of rapid growth can pose problems for a small firm, which may not yet have the personnel or resources to handle that level of success. Tumblr's surge in membership resulted in some initial stumbles, including a weekend when the whole site crashed, but the company was able to learn from its errors and work out the kinks in its performance.

than tripled in size. Between November 2010 and November 2011, Tumblr's total audience increased from 18.6 million users to 44 million.

Much of Tumblr's content consists of images and video, an important advantage for international users since there is no language barrier to overcome. Looking back on the company's growth during its first three years, it's apparent that Tumblr's success in the first year was driven by what are called "early adopters." Early adopters are consumers who eagerly embrace new technologies as soon as they become available. Increasing interest from international users characterized the company's second year. The third year was about mainstream domestic growth, which was when Tumblr became extremely popular in the United States. Part of what contributed to U.S. growth was that in the fall of 2009, students either starting college or those returning began to sign up for Tumblr in droves.

Tumblr also caught on with celebrities, many of whom had previously found an avid audience of fans ready to follow their tweets on Twitter. Some of the famous musicians and movie stars who started blogs on Tumblr include Britney Spears, Frank Ocean, Lady Gaga, Zooey Deschanel, and John Mayer. When Beyoncé and Jay-Z had their infant daughter, Blue Ivy Carter, they shared her baby pictures on Tumblr.

At the end of 2011, Mike Lazerow, the CEO of Buddy Media, made a prediction: "2012 will be the year of Tumblr." Once dismissed as a site that would appeal to only a small audience, Tumblr's influence is now acknowledged by the most powerful office in the world: the president of the United States. Barack Obama's campaign, which successfully harnessed the power of the Internet during the 2008 presidential election, included Tumblr in its reelection strategy. In October 2011, President Obama launched

President Barack Obama's successful bid for reelection in 2012 depended, in part, on his campaign's use of social media sites such as Tumblr.

his 2012 reelection campaign on Tumblr (with the slogan "Tumbling for change since 2011"), on a blog that encourages supporters to tell their stories on the site and be part of a "huge collaborative storytelling effort." The U.S. State Department maintains a tumblelog, as do major media organizations such as *Newsweek*, the *New York Times*, and the BBC. Without a doubt, Tumblr could run—or blog—with the big dogs.

CHAPTER 4

The Adjustment Period

In June 2011, Tumblr had a staff of thirty. By the following May, the company had more than tripled its headcount to 105. As a business grows, especially when it's dealing with dramatic growth, there are bound to be some adjustments as time goes on. Most successful Internet start-ups experience some type of growing pains—it's part of the natural evolution of a developing business. A company's continuing success depends on how well it can anticipate and respond to the various challenges that crop up along the way.

One of the first major staff changes at Tumblr was the departure of Marco Arment, the lead developer who had been part of Davidville since June 2006 and one-half of the two-person duo that launched the original version of Tumblr. One of Arment's side projects was a service called Instapaper. Instapaper allows you to save Web pages so that you can read them later. On September 10, 2010, in a post on his tumblelog, Arment resigned his position at Tumblr to devote all his time to Instapaper. In numerous interviews, Arment insisted that his departure was not due to any bad feelings between David Karp and himself, and that he would continue to play an active consulting role in the company.

Since its launch, image-heavy Tumblr had seemed a natural platform for the fashion industry. In October 2010, Rich Tong, a friend of David Karp's, was hired as Tumblr's fashion director. Some of Tong's duties involved

Fashion director Rich Tong resigned from Tumblr in December 2011 following complaints from the fashion industry that the service was charging huge fees to have its bloggers cover certain events.

reaching out to fashion brands and developing new features for fashion bloggers.

During New York's Fashion Week, one of the multibillion-dollar industry's largest events, Tumblr's bloggers covering the event were prominently featured. Large fashion brands, such as Ann Taylor, as well as start-ups, had invested heavily in the blogging platform. Then in October 2011, Tumblr, and Rich Tong in particular, found themselves at the center of a fashion-related fiasco. Word leaked out that Tumblr, in a proposal authored by Tong, was demanding outrageous amounts of money to blog about fashion events, an arrangement that struck many as unethical. Accusations were also made that Tumblr was playing favorites, charging certain brands for services while giving others custom products free of charge. The fashion community felt mistreated, and a lot of the industry's anger was aimed at Tong. On December 6, 2011, Tong resigned from his position at the company "to pursue other independent opportunities," as he explained on his tumblelog. Four months later, Valentine Uhovski came on board as Tumblr's new "fashion evangelist."

Another significant departure occurred in April 2012—John Maloney, the man who had once hired a very young David Karp to write code for the UrbanBaby Web site. Like Fred Seibert, for whom Karp had interned at Frederator Studios, Maloney had become an important mentor to Karp. In 2008, Karp had brought him on board as the New York–based president of Tumblr. However, the company was growing fast, and Maloney's skills as a general manager of a small business did not necessarily apply to what was swiftly becoming a large operation. As Karp put it, over time Maloney had essentially "hired himself out of a job." In his farewell post on the site, Maloney spoke

Tumblr and the "99 Percent"

On August 23, 2011, a New Yorker named Chris created a Tumblr account. A protest called Occupy Wall Street was planned for September 17 to speak out against the growing disparity between the rich and the poor in the United States, and Chris hoped to raise awareness about the event. On the tumblelog he created, called "We Are the 99 Percent," he asked readers to submit a photograph of themselves holding a sign that described their economic circumstances. Chris forgot about the blog until a few days later, when he logged back in and found his in-box overflowing with images that people had submitted.

One of those people was Priscilla Grim, an activist who offered to help Chris edit the blog, which soon was attracting more than a hundred submissions a day. One picture showed a man holding a sign that read: "I served in the U.S. Army. Served 16

The Occupy Wall Street movement, which flared up in New York City in the summer of 2011 and spread rapidly to different cities, called attention to socioeconomic inequalities in the United States.

months in Iraq. Now I deliver pizza. I am the 99%." Chris's blog went viral, and soon after, the Occupy Wall Street movement adopted "We Are the 99 Percent" as its slogan.

warmly about Karp and the Tumblr team and described the four years he spent at the company as "a pretty magical time."

Certain members of the company's original staff are still very much a part of today's Tumblr. Editorial director

Christopher Price (aka Topherchris) joined Tumblr the week after it launched in 2007 and is still an integral part of the team. Another employee who has been with the company for years is lead designer Peter Vidani. Vidani was an independent contractor who became a full-time staff member in 2009, heading up the department now called (with a nod to the Harry Potter books) the Ministry of Design.

NEW AND IMPROVED CREATIVE TOOLS

The swiftly multiplying number of people on staff wasn't the only change happening at Tumblr headquarters. David Karp and the other brains behind the site took user feedback seriously and never stopped thinking of ways to improve service. However, they were careful not to release a bunch of new features all at once because they wanted to keep the desktop (a blog's control panel) and the user experience as streamlined as possible.

Beginning in February 2009, Tumblr users could start sending audio posts from their phones. At the end of 2009, new tools that Tumblr introduced included an application programming interface (API) that allowed bloggers who were also on Twitter to interact with Tumblr at the same time, and "blog on the go." A new queue function let bloggers schedule the exact intervals when a series of posts would be published. The release of Tumblr versions in Japanese and German proved good news for international users. An additional security device was a backup tool that let you save everything on your blog to your hard drive. In January 2010, Tumblr added an Ask button that lets a person reading a blog ask the blogger a question.

Icons on a mobile phone identify many Internet services and sites, all of which fit right in the palm of your hand.

Beginning in June 2011, the blogging platform rolled out another series of new features designed to improve the site's performance and make it even more useful for its members. Tumblr introduced a feature that allowed people to respond privately to anyone sending a mes-

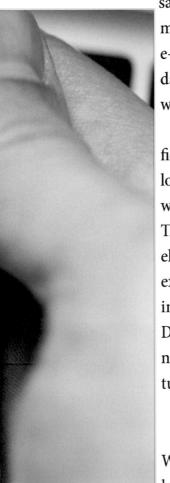

sage to their blog, which meant that Tumblr members could now use the site to exchange e-mail messages. The design of Tumblr's dashboard was streamlined, and new icons were added.

Not every new feature was an unqualified success, however. For every person who loved the new dashboard, there was someone who hated it and wanted the old one back. The team at Tumblr is just as determined to eliminate unnecessary features as it is to add excellent new ones, with the goal of keeping the platform as uncluttered as possible. David Karp has said proudly that for every new feature added to Tumblr, an older feature is removed.

BROWSER HACKS

When a new online service becomes popular, it is common for computer hackers to create software, called browser hacks, that extends the

Fans and Foes

Tumblr caught on quickly because people loved it and shared it with their friends. Fans of the service rave about how easy it is to use. The site appeals to techies who appreciate efficient design as well as creative people who don't consider themselves very tech savvy. The platform also wins supporters by trying to make the online experience a primarily positive one for its members. Tumblr lets users respond approvingly to other users' blogs or by prompting members to "Send Fan Mail" to one another.

If you've ever taken a look at any comments posted to the Web, you know that people can have very strong opinions online, and they don't always express themselves in the most respectful ways. One reason Tumblr doesn't allow users to post comments on other people's blogs is because this form of expression can become a source of negativity.

But people who aren't fans of Tumblr have had no trouble making their voices heard. Even before the infamous weekend when the service went dark, users were frustrated with slow performance and how much intermittent downtime Tumblr experienced, and they blasted the service for these failings. Like it or not, Tumblr has very quickly established itself as an addictive fixture of life online. It will be interesting to watch where it goes from here.

functions of a service. Then they make that software freely available to the public as a download. These unofficial extensions sometimes conflict with the legal agreements and requirements of the original service. They can also create problems for servers and staff of the original service and potentially introduce bugs and privacy risks, or so the service owners frequently claim. Critics respond that sites just want to block the public from using a tool that they didn't create and that, ultimately, they can't charge for.

In 2011, a Canadian engineer named Jeremy Cutler developed an unofficial browser extension called Missing e, a reference to the letter missing in Tumblr's name. The extension improved many of the microblogging platform's functions and enabled many new features. Included were a magnifier for photos and a way to hide images from the public, a tool for adding useful stuff to a Tumblr sidebar, various dashboard tweaks, and a Reblog Yourself function that improved reblogging of your own Tumblr posts. The extension quickly caught on, and by January 2012, Missing e had over three hundred thousand users.

But Tumblr wasn't happy about Missing e, and it wasn't long before users of the extension were greeted with a pop-up message when they logged onto Tumblr that warned them to stop using it. Tumblr also contacted Cutler and asked him to pull the extension offline and make a series of changes to it. Tumblr users who were fans of Missing e petitioned Tumblr to officially adopt the browser hack. Eventually, Tumblr agreed to adopt a more open attitude toward Missing e and other unofficial extensions, such as Tumblr Savior, Xkit, and Greasemonkey.

AN UNLIKELY CEO

The question of how to respond to browser hacks, and other key issues that arose during the first few years of Tumblr's life, represent the types of challenges that can make or break a company. David Karp proved that he was up to the task of providing stability and leadership when things turned rough. Mentors Fred Seibert and John Maloney were both impressed by their protégé's evolution as a leader. This gawky kid couldn't quite look them in the eye when they had first hired him. Yet he had transformed, in just a few short years, into the poised and articulate head of a company now valued at $800 million.

As chief executive officer of Tumblr, Karp has had to make many difficult decisions that could have had a huge impact on the future of the company: how much money

In frequent appearances on panels at industry conferences and at tech award events, David Karp (shown at the 16th Annual Webby Awards) sharpened his presenting skills as a spokesperson for Tumblr.

do we need to run this business? Whom do we want to finance us? How much control over the company do we want to retain? How many employees do we need today and how many will we need in six months? Should we sell now, or later, or never? Should we allow advertising on the site? It takes a person of rare ability to safely steer a start-up company through the turbulence of today's economy. Many people attend business school and still fail to launch a successful enterprise. It pays to remember that David Karp accomplished it all without so much as a high school diploma.

CHAPTER 5

Tumblr by the Numbers

When you visit the Tumblr home page, one of the first things you'll see is an "About" page tallying the current number of blogs, posts, and Tumblr employees. At the time of this writing, Tumblr boasted over 81 billion blogs, 36 billion posts, and 106 employees. The tally for that day's posts was 77,023,411, with the number of monthly page views at more than 17 billion: 17,189,566,464, to be precise. These numbers tell an interesting story about how Tumblr has evolved since the blogging platform was first launched in February 2007.

THE DEMOGRAPHICS

Marissa is a nineteen-year-old, single, white female in her freshman year at Santa Monica College in California. She's interested in the paranormal, and she started a Tumblr blog called the Haunted Surfshack, which features pictures of creepy places in Southern California and

People of all ages have embraced social media networks, but some sites, such as Tumblr, tend to attract a younger demographic of users.

reports of weird and unexplained local happenings. She's reblogged a bunch of other spooky blogs on her own site, and she's following a bunch more. Marissa's blog already has 847 followers, and when she hits 1,000 she'll be "Tumblr famous," as Tumblr popularity is sometimes called.

Numbers, specifically demographics, help describe the types of users that gravitate to Tumblr, fueling the service's escalating popularity. Based on available statistics, in the United States, more Tumblr members are female than male. Most are between the ages of eighteen and twenty-four, with the majority living in the Los Angeles area. Most users have college degrees, make less than $50,000 a year, and do not have children. Seventy-five percent are white, 10 percent are African American, and 5 percent are Asian.

As David Karp sees it, Tumblr users fall into three groups: the creators, the curators, and the consumers. The first group, who are honored by the service's current slogan, "Follow the world's creators," are the people who generate the original content that appears on the site. The second group, the curators, are those who sort through that content as well as material from outside the site, identify the best of it, and reblog it for the largest group of users, the consumers, or the Tumblr audience.

Tumblr Trivia

- Tumblr's user base generates about 55 million posts per day (that's 637 posts per second).
- The templates in Tumblr's Theme Garden numbered 1,300 and counting as of May 2012. Some of the most popular themes are Redux, Fluid, The Minimalist, Plaid, and One Very Important Thought.
- Tumblr had fewer features in 2012 than it did in 2011, a fact that makes CEO David Karp proud.
- In November 2009, Tumblr user Justin Johnson proposed to his girlfriend, Marissa Nystrom, via a Tumblr post. (Lucky for him, she said yes.) The post was reblogged and "liked" a total of 12,545 times, setting a record for most notes on a Tumblr post.
- As of June 22, 2012, the two most popular user-generated tags on Tumblr were the names of two boy bands: the British group One Direction, and Exo, a Chinese–South Korean band.

Another statistic you'll find on the Tumblr "About" page is the number of Tumblr meetups that have been held since the site was first launched. Tumblr users in a particular location can participate in a meetup, a social event where they can connect with other Tumblr users face-to-face. These gatherings may be large or small, and most are held in a restaurant or bar during happy hour on a weekday. Some meetups are organized around popular themes such as *Dr. Who* or anime. To date, the largest Tumblr meetup took place on June 5, 2011, in Curitiba, Brazil, with almost five hundred RSVPs. When users contact Tumblr about listing a meetup on the site, the service sends them materials that can be used to promote the event, such as stickers, name tags, and even tents. Organizers sometimes create their own meetup blogs.

THE DASHBOARD

The Tumblr dashboard is the private control panel that determines what appears on the public face of a blog. There you'll see seven icons prominently displayed, which represent the seven different kinds of media users can upload: text, photos, quotes, links, dialogue ("chat"), audio, and video. As of March 2012, according to *Wired* magazine, photos accounted for about 42 percent of all original posts on the site. The single largest category of content on Tumblr is fashion, which accounts for 16 percent of the material you'll find there.

Over the years, observers have seen a shift in the percentage of content on Tumblr derived from outside sources versus those inside the site itself. In the earliest stages of the service's development, the majority of material in the "Tumblrverse," or the Tumblr universe, originated from sources outside the platform. Partly as a result of the reblogging feature, more of the content on Tumblr has been recycled from inside the site over time. According to David Karp, every Tumblr post is reblogged an average of nine times.

AN INTERNATIONAL AUDIENCE

Because Tumblr's content consists mostly of images rather than words, it's been easy for users in other countries who may not speak English to adopt the service. International users initially had to rely on translation software to convert written text into their local language, which can be a clumsy and inaccurate process.

By November 2011, Tumblr had grown an astonishing 900 percent globally. As the international audience for the microblogging platform multiplied, Tumblr staff took steps to produce the service in additional languages. In the "About" section of its home page, Tumblr keeps track of the number of languages that the platform operates in, which in November 2012 was twelve. So far, in addition to English, Tumblr has been operating in French, German, Italian, Japanese, Polish, Russian, Spanish, Turkish, Portuguese, Brazilian Portuguese, and Dutch.

Tumblr Tuesdays

Each week, Tumblr randomly picks a handful of blogs to highlight on Tumblr Tuesday. Here are ten Tumblr blogs, from fun to informative, well worth reblogging:

1. EatSleepDraw: An online art gallery with images submitted by artists around the world.
2. All Creatures: For animal lovers, a collection of beautiful and fascinating photographs of all creatures, great and small.
3. Officials Say the Darndest Things: Curated by an organization of independent journalists, this blog serves up an impressive series of verbal bloopers uttered by elected officials.
4. Soup: This news blog, one of David Karp's favorites, is the creation of Anthony De Rosa, a man the *New York Times* calls "the undisputed king of Tumblr."
5. The Burning House: If your house was on fire, what would you grab to take with you? See user-submitted photos of what people hold precious.
6. It's Okay to Be Smart: An extremely entertaining science blog.

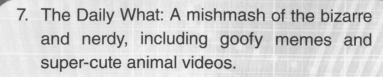

7. The Daily What: A mishmash of the bizarre and nerdy, including goofy memes and super-cute animal videos.

8. The Daily Dot: "The hometown newspaper of the World Wide Web" gathers news from other online sources and does its own reporting as well.

9. Sports Page: A collection of notable sports posts from Tumblr, all in one blog.

10. Pleated Jeans: Blogger and cartoonist Jeff Wysaski curates a hilarious collection of GIFs and other fun stuff.

MONEY MATTERS

A month after Tumblr first launched, when the number of employees added up to a grand total of two (namely, David Karp and Marco Arment), the site cost $5,000 a month to run. It takes plenty more than that to keep the service tumbling along today, since one employee's salary alone will likely cost the company more than that. Early on, venture capitalists invested many millions of dollars in the micro-blogging platform—$85 million, to be exact. Initially valued at $3 million, Tumblr's current estimated worth of $800 million is an increase of nearly 26,567 percent, or

Tumblr-like blogs can be used in creative ways. Writers Jessica Grose *(left)* and Doree Shafrir copublished a 2009 book called *Love, Mom* based on a blog featuring humorous e-mails from mothers to their adult children.

almost 267 times the amount of the original valuation. For comparison's sake, in the final round of investments in 2007, Facebook was valued at approximately $15 billion, so Tumblr's estimated value still falls far short of Facebook's high number. While Tumblr appears unlikely to attain the status of Facebook as a cultural and historical phenomenon, the blogging platform has undeniably made its mark on the Web and on digital culture.

FROM "BLOG" TO "TUMBLR"

After an epic sneeze, you don't usually ask a friend for a "facial tissue"—instead you ask her to "Hand me a Kleenex before I drip snot all over the keyboard!" Over time, a particular brand of tissue has become so popular that its name has effectively replaced the generic term, just as Band-Aid now stands for any self-stick bandage. One final, astonishing measure of Tumblr's popularity is the fact that according to projections based on Google data, by the end of 2012, online searches for "Tumblr" would outpace searches for the keyword "blog."

CHAPTER 6

Turning a Profit

Though Tumblr had been valued at $800 million, by the fall of 2011 the white-hot Internet start-up had never made a dime. Why would investors pour many millions of dollars into a company that had yet to prove that it could turn a profit? Venture capitalism, like gambling, always includes a significant element of risk. Tumblr investors were betting that their interest in the company would eventually pay off big time. But how? What was Tumblr's business model? People don't pay to use the service; you can set up as many blogs as you like on the site and it won't cost you a cent. So how does a business like Tumblr go about generating revenue?

WHAT'S YOUR PRICE?

One way that Internet start-ups make money is when larger companies purchase them. This is what happened to UrbanBaby, the Web site that David Karp helped John

From left: CEOs Charlie Kim (Next Jump), Karp, Nick Cannon (TeenNick), Susan Smith Ellis (Red), and Jim Cramer of CNBC at the Movers & Changers Forum during Global Entrepreneurship Week 2010.

Maloney run, which was purchased by a technology news site named CNET. Pyra Labs, the tiny company behind the development of Blogger (one of Tumblr's main competitors), sold that service to Google for an estimated $50

million in 2003. When Tumblr was gaining traction during its first three years, a number of companies approached David Karp. They offered him head-spinning amounts of money to sell his company. Accepting one of these offers would have made him a very rich young man. He could have retired at the age of twenty-four. But Karp was interested in other things besides merely accumulating wealth. He dreamed, instead, of turning Tumblr into a company like Apple that would continue creating beautiful and useful products for years to come. Yet, how exactly would he finance that dream? Karp and his team had to start thinking of creative ways to make money with Tumblr.

PREMIUM THEMES

One approach to raising money involved charging a percentage for the special templates available for purchase on the site. When you build a blog on Tumblr, you can

The Economics of Social Networks

In the course of its evolution, every social networking site has been faced with the problem of how to raise money. These services don't charge members to join the site or to use the network, so where does the cash come from? Facebook, Twitter, and LinkedIn have each found different solutions to this problem.

Facebook uses ads created by users, who pay for the ads to be displayed. Facebook also gets money from Microsoft for using Bing as its Web search feature.

Twitter uses Bing, too, and gets paid for it. The microblogging platform charges companies to feature their products in its Top Trends section. Twitter also makes money by licensing an exclusive live stream, called "the firehose," to Google and Microsoft for real-time Twitter search results. Analyzing this data gives these companies a good idea of what's trending, which they can use to their advantage when creating ads and designing products.

The professional networking site LinkedIn earns money by charging members for making certain connections within the network, such as services for job seekers or for hiring managers, and by charging market researchers to observe the network from the outside.

Finally, it's important to remember that making money isn't the same as making a profit. LinkedIn surpassed Wall Street's expectations and made money by May 2012, but Facebook and Twitter were still waiting to see if they would end the year profitably.

choose from a selection of templates available in the so-called Theme Garden, Tumblr's template library. Many themes are free to use, but there are also premium themes that can cost anywhere from $9 to $49. For a user who is trying to create a professional-looking blog that will stand out from the pack and eventually help him or her earn money, it may be a worthwhile investment to pay for a special theme. When theme designers add their designs to the Tumblr gallery, they agree to give the company a percentage of the fee they charge for each theme design. According to David Karp, some theme designers make tens of thousands of dollars a month. This win-win situation offers designers a place to advertise and sell their creations and generates money for the site as well.

Lionsgate movie studio's creative collaboration with Tumblr showcased the imaginative costumes of *The Hunger Games* characters, such as Effie Trinket, played by Elizabeth Banks.

PAID PROMOTIONS

Another way Tumblr has generated revenue is to let bloggers pay a small amount to promote their blog posts. If a user is already following a particular blog, a paid promotion will put a blogger's post at the top of a user's dashboard for twenty-four hours or until the user clicks a button to dismiss the post. Users who maintain a blog related to a business, or those who blog for a living, will naturally want to drive as much traffic as possible to their Web sites.

VALUABLE PARTNERSHIPS

As Karp would be among the first to tell you, Tumblr seems to inspire creativity in those who use it. The various tools that the site makes available to individual users have been put to good use by larger organizations as well.

Early on, *Newsweek* and the *New York Times* each adopted the blogging platform to build well-designed tumblelogs. One of the most creative marketing partnerships of 2012 occurred between Tumblr and Lionsgate studio, distributor of the 2012 film *The Hunger Games*, based on the best-selling book series. To whet fans' appetites for the film's release, Lionsgate created a Tumblr blog called Capitol Couture. The site speaks to a fictionalized audience of citizens from the dystopian world of the book and features fantastic fashions created exclusively for the

"Net" Worth

By most estimates, David Karp's personal wealth in 2012 was about $40 million. That may seem like a ton of money to most of us, but it puts him at the bottom of the following list of entrepreneurs who have made their fortunes on the Net:

Naveen Seladurai, Foursquare: $80 million
Angelo Sotira, DeviantArt: $87 million
Blake Ross, Firefox: $150 million
Matt Mullenweg, WordPress: $250 million
Gurbaksh Singh Chahal, GWallet: $300 million
Drew Houston, Dropbox: $600 million
Dustin Moscowitz, Facebook: $3.5 billion
Andrew Mason, Groupon: $4.75 billion
Mark Zuckerberg, Facebook: $12.1 billion

movie by real-life designers such as Alexander McQueen. Capitol Couture was part of a skillfully executed marketing campaign that helped *The Hunger Games* smash box-office records.

The Cartoon Network and the BBC TV series *Dr. Who* have also found innovative and entertaining ways to promote their products on Tumblr, by encouraging fans to share their photos, art, and stories related to their shows. Sponsoring more partnerships with billion-dollar industries such as television, film, and fashion could definitely be a valuable source of revenue for Tumblr.

ADVERTISING

In early discussions about how to generate money with Tumblr, the subject of advertising often came up. Businesses ranging from television programming to taxi cab companies to sports teams and daily newspapers could not function without the funding that advertisers provide. It was natural to assume that Tumblr would take advantage of the same opportunities. With the blogging platform's audience of millions and counting, national brands could put their ads in front of a lot of eyeballs, and they were ready to pay handsomely for that privilege.

Advertising, though it surrounds us and is an accepted aspect of our daily life, can frequently be intrusive and annoying. An example of this may be when you can't help but notice the prominently placed logo for a sports car featured in a blockbuster movie. Karp hated the way that the banner and pop-up ads featured on YouTube and Facebook intruded on the user experience. When asked during an April 2010 interview with the *Los Angeles Times* about the possibility of selling ads on Tumblr, Karp said, "We're pretty opposed to advertising. It really turns our stomachs."

Moving Pictures

One creative form of advertising that has already created a stir in the Tumblrverse makes use of a new visual medium called a cinemagraph, a still photograph in which a minor and repeated movement occurs. The term "cinemagraph" was coined by visual graphics artist Kevin Burg and his partner, photographer Jamie Beck, who helped popularize the new art form on her Tumblr blog, From Me to You. A cross between a still image and a video, a cinemagraph is similar to an animated GIF. However, whereas animated GIFs produce a 3-D effect by animating the whole frame with a fast, recurring action, in a cinemagraph only a portion of the frame is animated, creating a far more sophisticated and subtle effect. For example, an ad for the 2012 film *Beasts of the Southern Wild* featured a cinemagraph of the film's young protagonist in which all that moves is her hair, blowing gently in the wind. Cinemagraphs now appear online in everything from fashion spreads to cola ads.

Those were words that Karp would come to regret. In subsequent interviews, he would have to do some backpedaling and clarify that he wasn't opposed to all advertising, just ads that weren't conceived and produced in a creative way. Clearly, the Tumblr team had decided to rethink the company's official position on advertising as a potential source of revenue. By May 2012, the industry news buzzed with stories—featuring plenty of cracks about the condition of David Karp's stomach—announcing that Tumblr would start accepting ads after all.

The type of advertising Karp decided he could embrace was something he called creative brand advertising, which harked back to the golden age of the business. In the 1950s and 1960s, times portrayed in the popular *Mad Men* television series, the most successful and memorable ad campaigns were those that told stories that engaged and seduced the consumer. In contrast, today's online ads often alienate and frustrate consumers when they expand on the page and block content or feature annoying animated GIFs or pop-ups. Karp believed that advertisers should be forced to be as creative as the members of the Tumblr community. He also stressed that he wanted a portion of the advertising space, or "real estate," on Tumblr to be available to the creators using the site and not just the big brands outside of it.

Currently, the service maintains two designated areas, Tumblr Radar and Tumblr Spotlight, where members can find content outside their networks and where advertisers as well as users can pay to sponsor posts. Tumblr Radar features a selection of site highlights curated by Tumblr

Major brands that wanted to purchase advertising space on Tumblr included multinational companies such as Adidas, manufacturer of athletic gear.

editors that appears adjacent to members' dashboards. So does Tumblr Spotlight, though David Karp has stressed his intention to keep the dashboard itself an ad-free zone. Advertising space in the Radar and Spotlight sections sells for $25,000 and up. Tumblr has signed on a number of sponsors, including big brands such as Coca-Cola, Adidas, MTV, and Calvin Klein. In September 2012, Tumblr further demonstrated its commitment to advertising when it hired Lee Brown, formerly of Yahoo! and the daily deal site Groupon, as the company's first head of global sales.

Premium themes, paid promotions, creative partner-ships with other industries, and innovative advertising are all key components of a revenue-generating plan that David Karp anticipates will begin earning money for the company in 2013. Since microblogging networks have so far not been profit-making operations, plenty of eyes will be watching closely to see whether Tumblr's financial plan actually pays off.

CHAPTER 7

The Future of the Company

Tumblr's headquarters are situated in Manhattan, in the historic Flatiron District, at the heart of New York's Silicon Alley. The office is split between two floors, with most of the staff occupying the top floor, and the bottom floor designated for social and meeting areas. Bike racks behind the reception area are provided for those employees who brave the vehicle-snarled city streets to commute by bicycle to work. Most of Tumblr's more than one hundred employees don't work in individual cubicles, but at long tables covered with impressive tangles of wires, with no physical barriers between workspaces. Each workspace usually features two computer screens—typically a large computer screen and a laptop—and a twenty-something white male tapping away at one of the two keyboards.

The kitchen in the middle of the office contains a refrigerator plastered with letters from Tumblr fans, and art created by Tumblr users brightens the office walls. The employee bathrooms feature Tumblrbots, the company's cute, robotic cartoon icons, designating the men's and women's rooms. Downstairs you'll find a Ping-Pong table, and there's usually a partially completed jigsaw puzzle spread out across one of the coffee tables. An eleven-year-old Pomeranian named Tommy, which the office adopted, has become the Tumblr mascot. The playful atmosphere of Tumblr headquarters may help explain why David Karp lists Willy Wonka, the fictional CEO in Roald Dahl's classic book *Charlie and the Chocolate Factory*, among his heroes.

SHOULD TUMBLR BE FREE?

When David Karp first envisioned Tumblr, one of the things he wanted to do was give users the freedom to be as creative as they desired. At first, Tumblr was open to allowing users to upload all types of content. The service made it super easy to add images, audio and video, or anything else a user wanted to post on her or his blog. Karp trusted that users would respect their blog space and flag any inappropriate content. He believed that this form of self-policing would ensure that the Tumblr online community remained a healthy and supportive one.

Yet, the Internet is a big place. While Karp and others may disagree about the exact percentage of such content,

David Karp and industry writer Jason Kincaid engage in conversation at TechCrunch Disrupt 2011, a major technology conference held in a different city each year.

one doesn't have to look far on Tumblr to find inappropriate images. Some are labeled NSFW, or "Not Safe (or Suitable) for Work," and will be screened out if you have this type of filter set on your browser, but others may not be—the labeling is left up to the user who posts the image.

Internet watchdogs began to find sites on Tumblr that appeared to promote dangerous behaviors such as cutting and starving oneself, and abusing laxatives. They also found blogs that seemed to encourage suicide. These groups began pressuring Tumblr and other social networks to ban this type of content from the blogging platform.

In March 2012, following the lead of other social media sites such as Facebook, Twitter, and the video-sharing site YouTube, Tumblr began removing blogs that appeared to promote self-harm and eating disorders such as anorexia and bulimia. The service's guidelines now instruct members not to post "content that actively promotes or glorifies self-harm." While groups such as Beat, an eating disorder support organization, celebrated this move, others argued that removing such blogs would actively limit people's freedom of speech. Critics also expressed concern that the new policy would essentially penalize people for sharing their thoughts and feelings in online forums, and therefore damage the support community that had gathered around such topics. An online petition signed by nearly two thousand people urged Tumblr to stop removing the blogs.

In the aftermath of the Aurora, Colorado, theater shooting that killed twelve moviegoers and wounded fifty-nine others at a July 2012 premiere of the Batman movie *The Dark Knight Rises*, many people were horrified when an online fan club of self-professed "Holmies" sprang up on Tumblr in support of the shooter, James Holmes. Certainly, anyone who has taken a tour of the Tumblrverse knows that it isn't hard to find blogs that many would consider deeply offensive. However, does that mean Tumblr should begin actively policing its site?

What exactly constitutes free speech is an age-old question that continues to be debated in today's culture. Rapidly developing technologies frequently outstrip a society's capacity to create rules and expectations related to the use of those new technologies, which is why laws have only recently been passed regulating cell phone use while driving. Questions of Internet freedom versus online censorship will be discussed and argued about in the years to come.

COPYRIGHT ISSUES

In its continuing evolution, the Internet has increasingly enabled users to share various kinds of content with one another. Tumblr added a feature that encourages users to attribute the source of any image they post on their blogs, but people don't always give credit where credit is due. Photo-sharing sites such as Tumblr and Flickr have come under fire for allowing users to share images that they are legally required to pay for, a crime known as copyright infringement. According to the Digital Millennium Copyright Act (DMCA), services such as these that host user-generated content usually are not liable for prosecution for copyright infringement if they agree to remove the material when requested to do so.

Possibly as part of a strategy to avoid copyright issues, in 2012, Tumblr took steps to increase the amount of original material on the site by hiring more original content producers. Many of these staff members will be responsible for unearthing interesting content from the platform's millions of members and telling the stories of creative Tumblr users.

PARTNERSHIPS

Before Tumblr came on the scene, the most popular blog-hosting platforms were WordPress and Blogger. Like Tumblr, each service is free and easy to use, and allows some degree of customization. However, Karp thought the existing blogging platforms served writers better than they did visual artists.

A growing number of Tumblr users, especially first-time bloggers, clearly agreed. As the service evolved to combine features of a microblogging platform and a social network, Tumblr also seemed to be positioning itself to compete with Facebook and Twitter. However, Karp has taken pains to point out that he is interested in integration, not competition.

Twitter shares investors with Tumblr, after all, which suggests that David Karp is not the only person who believes there is plenty of room on the Internet for everyone. The Tumblr settings enable users to integrate with Twitter, and Facebook to share posts with these social networks. Matt Mullenweg, the founder of WordPress, has stressed that he also sees his platform and Tumblr as complementary services. In June 2012, Mullenweg announced that WordPress was adding a feature that would allow users to instantly share their blog posts on Tumblr.

David Karp's and Matt Mullenweg's emphasis on complementing rather than competing with each other reflects a key characteristic of Web 2.0—the drive to enable sharing and collaboration online, and to knock down walls that might impede the free flow of information. In 2008, a blogging platform called Posterous was launched. The simplicity of the service rivaled Tumblr's, and it occupied the same niche between Twitter's 140-character limit and traditional longer blog posts. Twitter acquired Posterous in 2012.

Where Posterous distinguished itself was in the depth of its integration with other existing social networks. Even people who weren't yet members could post all types of content on Posterous via e-mail. Another service developed after Tumblr that made a big splash on the Web is Pinterest, a social photo-sharing site launched in 2010.

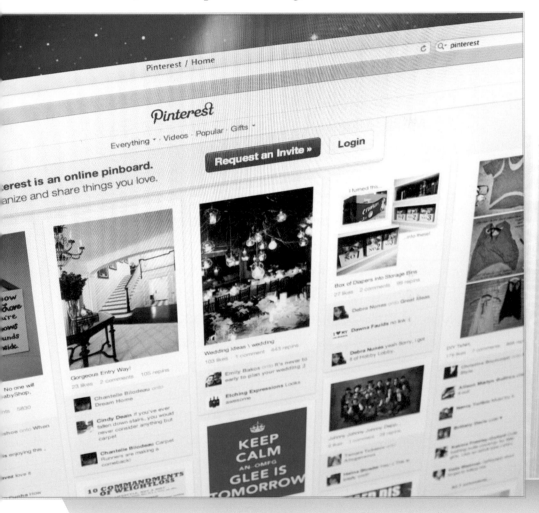

The trend on the most recent social networks, such as Pinterest (http://www .pinterest.com), is toward integration, making it easier for users to share content with any number of Internet platforms.

The Facebook IPO: A Cautionary Tale

In the weeks before Facebook's highly anticipated IPO (initial public offering), its shares were valued at $38 each, which had the potential to earn the company $18.4 billion. On May 18, 2012, Facebook debuted on the NASDAQ stock exchange, where all trading is done electronically. Shares for many of the world's largest technology companies, including Apple, Microsoft, Amazon, eBay, and Google, are traded on the NASDAQ. Wearing his signature hoodie and surrounded by cheering employees, a grinning Mark Zuckerberg stood in Facebook's Palo Alto headquarters and rang the opening bell that would start trading.

Unfortunately, things did not unfold as planned. Electronic glitches caused delays in trading, and millions of dollars were wrongly placed. Five hundred million shares changed hands, but the price of the shares began to fall and continued to sink in the days that followed. Facebook's much-hyped IPO, one of the largest in the history of the Internet, turned into a major bust. Brokers pointed fingers at NASDAQ, and more than forty lawsuits were filed. Facebook lost more than $10 billion in value, and investors wondered about the company's revenue potential.

Facebook's massive IPO nosedive proved a sobering and instructive lesson for other Internet start-ups. David Karp and other Web entrepreneurs watched closely to see what they could learn and what lessons might be applied to their own companies. When and if Tumblr goes public, the Facebook IPO will provide the playbook for what can go wrong.

Members create a virtual pin board, where they organize and share things they find online. A lot of the content on Pinterest actually originates on Tumblr. Services such as Posterous and Pinterest attract many of the same users as Tumblr, but increasingly people utilize many different platforms and publish their posts in multiple places at once.

In 2012, Tumblr also integrated with a service called Spotify, a Swedish music-streaming service that offers free access to a huge library of music from all over the world. Tumblr members who post audio on their blogs can now post any song available on Spotify. This integration lets Tumblr users search for a specific musical track or a band, and they can even post an entire playlist on their tumblelogs.

Another characteristic of Web 2.0 is an Internet that can be accessed anytime, anywhere. Statistics show that people spend twice as much time on their mobile phones as they do eating each day. Mobile Internet usage is on track to overtake desktop Internet usage by 2014, and Karp wants to make sure that the increasing number of smartphone users can easily access Tumblr on the go. The service integrates with mobile platforms via the applications (or apps) it has designed for the Apple and Android operating systems.

A FUND-RAISING TOOL

During its third year of operations, Tumblr gained the ability to accept payments online. In response to the massive BP oil spill that spewed millions of gallons of oil into the Gulf of Mexico in 2010, Tumblr painted its blue dashboard oil-slick black and added a feature that let users donate to various environmental groups working to clean up the gulf. The service has solicited donations from users in response to natural disasters, such as the devastating earthquake and tsunami that struck Japan in 2011. Tumblr has also advocated for social causes. An anti-gay-bullying

effort on the site aimed to raise both funds and aware-ness. The growing size of the Tumblr audience means that fund-raising requests reach millions of people, resulting in much-needed donations for worthy causes.

Internet fund-raising efforts in response to global disasters, such as the 2011 earthquake and tsunami in Japan, can swiftly reach out to everyone in the global online community.

WHAT'S NEXT FOR TUMBLR?

One of Karp's responsibilities as CEO of Tumblr is to give interviews with various media organizations and answer questions about his company. One question that kept coming up concerned whether or not Tumblr would one day "go public," or sell shares of the company to the public in what's called an IPO, or initial public offering.

Going public is a two-stage process. First, the company's underwriters (those who assume the organization's financial risks, such as investment bankers) buy shares directly from the company at the IPO price. Then they turn around and sell shares at that price to their own clients—often mutual funds, hedge funds, and institutional investors. This happens in the evening, and on the next day those who purchased IPO shares can turn around and sell them to the public on the open market.

The Digital Millennium Copyright Act

The rapid-fire growth of the Internet has often outstripped efforts to regulate its use. The Digital Millennium Copyright Act is an example of legislation playing catch-up with technological innovation. Signed into law by President Bill Clinton in October 1998, the DCMA intends to stop "Internet piracy" by restraining and eliminating illegal downloads and file sharing. The act makes it a crime to produce or share technology, devices, and services designed to bypass measures that control access to copyrighted works. The DMCA also includes what is known as a safe harbor provision. This provision limits the liability of services that host user-generated content. Services such as Tumblr usually cannot be held responsible and prosecuted if they agree to remove certain copyrighted material when they receive a DMCA takedown notice requesting them to do so. A takedown notice is a warning to a Web-hosting company or a search engine that it is either hosting or linking to copyright-infringing material. Web hosts must remove or disable access to the material, while search engines have to stop linking to it.

In 2007, the global mass media conglomerate Viacom filed a $1 billion lawsuit against YouTube and its parent company, Google, claiming that the video-sharing site was engaging in "massive intentional copyright infringement." In its defense, YouTube relied on the safe harbor provision of the DMCA to shield itself from liability. The court's initial ruling in favor of YouTube was subsequently appealed by Viacom.

The timing of an IPO is crucial. Many Internet start-ups are justifiably nervous about what will happen when and if they decide to go public. Underwriters can easily overvalue companies, and stock exchanges may not be able to handle large volumes of trading. This was the case when Facebook went public. If Karp decides it's time for a Tumblr IPO, he will have to avoid making the same mistakes.

As Tumblr continues to grow and evolve, Karp will have a lot more responsibility riding on his shoulders. He says that showing up and being a good leader for people is incredibly hard—all the pressure has caused him many sleepless nights. He relaxes by riding his motorcycle, taking photographs, and spending time with his girlfriend, Rachel Eakley. When he's away from the office, Karp makes sure to take a break from the Internet because being online all the time makes him feel "gross."

When asked about his personal heroes, David Karp often mentions Steve Jobs, the visionary head of Apple Inc., who died of pancreatic cancer in October 2011. Karp grew up totally obsessed with Jobs's business acumen, displayed at his famous keynote speeches when he would unveil the latest Apple product before a rapt audience. Like Jobs, who dropped out of Reed College during his freshman year, Karp has had little use for formal education. Karp also seems to have an instinct for creating high-tech

David Karp, speaking here at the 2012 Digital Life Design conference in Munich, Germany, contributes to an ongoing global conversation about what the digital future holds for us all.

tools that people desire for their beauty and utility. Jobs and Willy Wonka, another one of Karp's role models, each built a factory that produces amazing things. It's not hard to imagine, when he finally does manage to get some sleep, what David Karp dreams about.

Fact Sheet on

DAVID KARP

Nickname: Tumblr Daddy

Birth Date: July 6, 1986

Birthplace: New York City

Education: Attended Bronx Science High School through ninth grade, then was homeschooled. Has not completed his high school diploma.

First Job: Summer internship at Frederator Studios

Current Title: Founder and CEO of Tumblr

Current Residence: Williamsburg section of Brooklyn, New York, in a building that is a former shoe polish factory

Marital Status: In a relationship with Rachel Eakley

Favorite Outfit: A patterned shirt, a hoodie sweatshirt, dark pants, and white Converse Jack Purcell sneakers

Net Worth: $40 million

Vehicle of Choice: Black Triumph Bonneville motorcycle

Go-to Tech Device: iPad

Favorite TV Shows: *30 Rock*, *The Daily Show*, *The Colbert Report*, *Futurama*, *The Office*

Pet: A French-English bulldog mix named Clark

Quote: "As long as I'm able to create, I'll be happy at Tumblr." (Interview with *Business Insider*, January 5, 2012)

Fact Sheet on

TUMBLR

Year Launched: 2007

Founded by: David Karp, with Marco Arment

Original Name: Tumblehub

Original Slogan: "Blogging Made Easy"

Current Slogan: "Follow the World's Creators"

Headquarters: New York City

CEO: David Karp

Company Mascot: Tommy, an eleven-year-old Pomeranian

Number of Employees: 106 (as of November 17, 2012)

Number of Blogs Created: Over 81 million

Number of Monthly Page Views: Nearly 18 million

Number of Languages Tumblr is Localized in: 12

Value: $800 million

1986: David Karp is born on July 6 in New York City.

1997: Karp teaches himself the HTML coding language.

2000: Karp becomes an intern at Frederator Studios, Fred Seibert's cartoon production company in Manhattan.

2001: Karp drops out of prestigious Bronx Science High School to be homeschooled. He registers the Internet domain name for his own consulting company, Davidville.

2002: John Mahoney hires Karp as a programmer at UrbanBaby, a Web site for hip urban moms.

2003: At the age of seventeen, Karp moves to Tokyo, Japan, for five months, where he continues working as the CTO (chief technology officer) of UrbanBaby. They do not know he is in Japan, or that he is only seventeen.

2006: UrbanBaby is sold to CNET for an undisclosed amount. Karp hires Marco Arment as an engineer for Davidville.

2007: Tumblr launches on February 19. Within the first two weeks, seventy-five thousand people join the service. Six months later, the reblog button is added to the Tumblr dashboard. Karp and Arment stop taking clients to focus on Tumblr.

Timeline

2008: In its first round of raising money, Tumblr pulls in $750,000. In the second round, the company generates $4.5 million in investments.

2009: David Karp is named Best Young Tech Entrepreneur by *BusinessWeek* magazine.

2010: David Karp is named to the MIT Technology Review TR35 as one of the top thirty-five innovators in the world under age thirty-five. Marco Arment leaves Tumblr to focus on Instapaper. Tumblr goes dark on December 6 when a shortage of servers can't handle all the traffic on the site. Service cannot be restored in some areas until more than twenty-four hours later.

2011: President Barack Obama's campaign team launches a tumblelog for his 2012 reelection efforts. Tumblr raises $85 million in venture capital and is valued at $800 million. The company triples in size.

2012: John Maloney resigns as president. "Tumblr" surpasses the keyword "blog" in online searches.

Glossary

angel investor A wealthy individual who invests his or her own money in a business, sometimes for personal reasons.

animated GIF A graphic image on a Web page that moves repeatedly. GIF (pronounced "jiff") stands for Graphics Interchange Format.

beta version An early version of a computer program that has not yet been tested for bugs.

blog A chronological online log of information kept by an individual, a group, or a business. The term is a merging of the terms "web" and "log."

blogosphere The collective community of all blogs and bloggers around the world.

computer hacking When someone modifies hardware or software in a way that alters the creator's original intent.

dashboard The private control panel of a blog, where users establish the settings for the blog's appearance and content.

early adopter A person who starts using a product or technology as soon as it becomes available.

hashtag A word or phrase prefixed with the symbol "#"; also, a short message posted on a microblogging network such as Twitter.

HTML Hypertext markup language; the text formatting code used to build Web pages.

icon A graphic symbol (usually a simple picture) that represents an object or a program on a computer's hard drive. Icons are one of the fundamental features of graphical user interface (GUI) and help make computers user friendly.

Internet start-up A technology-oriented online company in the early stages of development.

link Short for hyperlink; a link is a navigation tool that allows a user to go from one Web page to another by clicking the link.

meetup A hosted gathering of Internet users; a social event where can they meet one another in person.

microblog A blog made up of extremely brief text or multimedia posts.

post A publication to a blog, possibly containing text, images, or other media.

share An equal, usually small, part of a company's stock.

tag A keyword assigned to a piece of information, such as an image, a blog entry, or a video clip, that enables online information to be organized for easy searching. Tags are usually assigned by the content creator or online community.

tumblelog A blog hosted by Tumblr; a tumblelogger is a blogger on Tumblr.

Tumblr famous A blogger is known as "Tumblr famous" once his or her blog attracts one thousand followers.

venture capital Private funding used to support new businesses with the potential for high growth. Venture capitalists are professional investors.

WYSIWYG An acronym for What You See Is What You Get, a system where the content during editing looks very similar to the end result.

The Alice Project
Carnegie Mellon University
Computer Science Department
Pittsburgh, PA 15213-3891
(412) 268-2565
Web site: http://www.alice.org
The Alice Project is a suite of educational software developed by Carnegie Mellon University that teaches the basics of computer programming using a 3-D environment. Alice was designed to appeal specifically to girls, who are underrepresented in computer programming courses. However, the software can be used by anyone. Alice 3.1 is currently available in both English and Spanish, and is free to download.

Canadian Advanced Technology Alliance (CATA)
207 Bank Street, Suite 416
Ottawa, ON K2P 2N2
Canada
(613) 236-6550
Web site: http://www.cata.ca

The Canadian Advanced Technology Alliance is a comprehensive resource for the latest high-tech news and the largest high-tech association in Canada.

Electronic Privacy Information Center
1718 Connecticut Avenue NW, Suite 200
Washington, DC 20009
(202) 483-1140
Web site: http://www.epic.org
The Electronic Privacy Information Center is an organization dedicated to examining civil liberty issues that relate to the Internet.

GetNetWise
Internet Education Foundation
1634 Eye Street NW
Washington, DC 20006
(202) 638-4370
Web site: http://www.getnetwise.org
GetNetWise is a public service sponsored by Internet industry corporations and public interest organizations dedicated to making sure that Internet users have positive, safe, and secure online experiences.

MediaSmarts
950 Gladstone Avenue, Suite 120
Ottawa, ON K1Y 3E6

Canada

(800) 896-3342

Web site: http://www.mediasmarts.ca

MediaSmarts is a Canadian not-for-profit organization for digital and media literacy, with helpful resources on these subjects. The organization's work falls into the areas of education, public awareness, and research and policy.

New York Tech Meetup

175 Varick Street

New York, NY 10014

Web site: http://www.nytm.org

Founded in 2004, NY Tech Meetup has nearly twenty-six thousand members, made up of professionals from all parts of the New York technology community. (You must be eighteen to join.) The organization sponsors monthly events featuring talks and product demos and has been central to the rebirth of New York's Silicon Alley.

OpenMedia

1424 Commercial Drive

P.O. Box 21674

Vancouver, BC V5L 5G3

Canada

(604) 633-2744

Web site: http://www.openmedia.ca

OpenMedia.ca is a Canadian grassroots organization that safeguards the possibilities of the open and affordable Internet.

TrevorSpace

The Trevor Project

9056 Santa Monica Boulevard, Suite 208

West Hollywood, CA 90069

(310) 271-8845

(866) 488-7386

Web site: http://www.trevorspace.com

TrevorSpace is a social networking site for lesbian, gay, bisexual, transgender, and questioning youth ages thirteen through twenty-four and their friends and allies. This monitored site is free to join.

Tumblr

35 East 21st Street, #6E

New York, NY 10010

(678) HEY-TUMBLR (439-8862)

Web site: http://www.tumblr.com

Tumblr is a social blogging site.

Young Entrepreneur

Entrepreneur Media, Inc.

2445 McCabe Way, Suite 400

Irvine, CA 92614

(949) 261-2325

Web site: http://www.youngentrepreneur.com

Launched in 1999, Young Entrepreneur is one of the largest online forum communities for entrepreneurs worldwide. The site includes a blog, how-to articles, and the latest entrepreneurial news and information.

WEB SITES

Due to the changing nature of Internet links, Rosen Publishing has developed an online list of Web sites related to the subject of this book. This site is updated regularly. Please use this link to access the list:

http://www.rosenlinks.com/IBIO/Tumb

For Further Reading

Banks, Michael A. *Blogging Heroes: Interviews with 30 of the World's Top Bloggers*. Hoboken, NJ: Wiley Publishing, 2008.

Cook, Colleen Ryckert. *Frequently Asked Questions About Social Networking* (Teen Life). New York, NY: Rosen Publishing, 2011.

Crowder, David. *Building a Web Site for Dummies*. Hoboken, NJ: Wiley Publishing, 2010.

Farrell, Mary. *Computer Programming for Teens*. Boston, MA: Thomas Course Technology, 2008.

Freedman, Jeri. *Careers in Computer Science and Programming*. New York, NY: Rosen Classroom, 2011.

Gardner, Susannah, and Shane Birley. *Blogging for Dummies*. Hoboken, NJ: Wiley Publishing, 2012.

Goldsworthy, Steve. *Steve Jobs* (Remarkable People). New York, NY: AV2 by Weigl, 2011.

Hansen, Mark Victor. *The Richest Kids in America: How They Earn It, How They Spend It, How You Can Too*. Newport Beach, CA: Hansen House, 2009.

Hillstrom, Laurie Collier. *Online Social Networks*. Farmington Hills, MI: Lucent Books 2010.

Hussey, Tris. *Create Your Own Blog: 6 Easy Projects to Start Blogging Like a Pro*. Indianapolis, IN: Sams, 2010.

Livingston, Jessica. *Founders at Work: Stories of Startups' Early Days*. Berkeley, CA: Apress, 2007.

Lohr, Steve. *Digital Revolutionaries: The Men and Women Who Brought Computing to Life*. New York, NY: Flash Point, 2009.

Lusted, Marcia Amidon. *Mark Zuckerberg: Facebook Creator* (Essential Lives). Edina, MN: ABDO Publishing Company, 2012.

Lusted, Marcia Amidon. *Social Networking: MySpace, Facebook, & Twitter* (Technology Pioneers). Edina, MN: ABDO Publishing Company, 2012.

Marques, Marcelo. *Hackerteen: Volume 1: Internet Blackout*. Sebastopol, CA: O'Reilly, 2009.

Mason, Margaret. *No One Cares What You Had for Lunch: 100 Ideas for Your Blog*. Berkeley, CA: Peachpit Press, 2009.

Obee, Jennifer. *Social Networking: The Ultimate Teen Guide*. Lanham, MD: Scarecrow Press, 2012.

Raatma, Lucia. *Social Networks* (21st Century Skills). Ann Arbor, MI: Cherry Lake Publishing, 2010.

Rosenberg, Scott. *Say Everything: How Blogging Began, What It's Becoming, and Why It Matters*. New York, NY: Three Rivers Press, 2009.

Ryan, Peter K. *Social Networking*. New York, NY: Rosen Publishing, 2011.

Whiting, Jim. *Online Communication and Social Networking* (Issues in the Digital Age). San Diego, CA: ReferencePoint Press, 2011.

Zandt, Deanna. *Share This! How You Will Change the World with Social Networking.* San Francisco, CA: Berrett-Koehler Publishers, 2010.

Bibliography

Brian, Matt. "Tumblr Crosses 20 Billion Post Mark." *USA Today*, March 8, 2012. Retrieved July 28, 2012 (http://www.usatoday.com/tech/news/story/2012-03-28/tumblr-growth/53825266/1).

Cheshire, Tom. "Tumbling on Success." *Wired* (UK), February 12, 2012. Retrieved July 22, 2012 (http://www.wired.co.uk/magazine/archive/2012/03/features/tumbling-on-success?page=all).

Dana, Rebecca. "Tumblr's Growing Pains: Can the Blogging Site Cash In?" *Newsweek*, April 30, 2012. Retrieved July 22, 2012(http://www.thedailybeast.com/newsweek/2012/04/29/tumblr-plans-to-cash-in-will-53-million-bloggers-agree.html).

Dixon, Chris. "Interview with David Karp." *Huffington Post*, December 27, 2011. Retrieved July 20, 2012 (http://videos.huffingtonpost.com/tech/tumblrs-david-karp-interview-517158474).

Edelsburg, Natan. "How TV Can Leverage Tumblr for Social Buzz and Analysis." Lost Remote, May 31, 2012. Retrieved August 4, 2012 (http://www.lostremote.com/2012/05/31/how-tv-can-leverage-tumblr-for-social-buzz).

Edwards, Jim. "Tumblr Wants $25,000 Per Ad—Here's
What They Look Like." *Business Insider*, May 2, 2012.
Retrieved July 22, 2012 (http://articles.businessinsider
.com/2012-05-02/news/31531112_1_blog-twitter
-advertisers).

Evans, Teri. "Tumblr's David Karp Learned 4 Lessons
from Last Year's Massive Network Failure." *Business
Insider*, May 25, 2011. Retrieved July 19, 2012 (http://
tech.topicsky.com/clickout/851).

Halliday, John. "David Karp, Founder of Tumblr, on
Realising His Dream." *Guardian* (UK), January 29,
2012. Retrieved August 3, 2012 (http://www.guardian
.co.uk/media/2012/jan/29/tumblr-david-karp
-interview).

Jeffries, Adrianne. "This Is Why Your Tumblr's Down."
BetaBeat, April 25, 2011. Retrieved July 22, 2012
(http://betabeat.com/2011/04/welcome-to-davidville
-turbulence-at-tumblr-tests-tempers-as-start-up-scales
-success).

Little, Lyneka. "Tumblr's David Karp on Why NYC Beats
Silicon Valley." *Young Entrepreneur*, May 17, 2012.
Retrieved June 29, 2012 (http://www.youngentrepreneur
.com/blog/tumblrs-david-karp-on-why-nyc-beats-
silicon-valley).

Loten, Angus "Can Tumblr Turn a Profit?" *Wall Street
Journal*, May 16, 2012. Retrieved July 24, 2012 (http://

online.wsj.com/article/SB10001424052702303505504
577406432743682976.html).

Martin, J. Quinn. "The 21-Year-Old Behind a Darling
New York Web Startup." *New York Sun*, November 8,
2001. Retrieved July 19, 2012 (http://www.nysun.co
m/business/21-year-old-behind-a-darling-new-york
-web-startup/66108).

Mashable. "Tumblr Numbers: The Rapid Rise of Social
Blogging." November 2011. Retrieved June 30,
2012 (http://mashable.com/2011/11/14/tumblr
-infographic).

Pepitone, Julianne. "Facebook IPO: What the %$#!
Happened?" CNN Money, May 23, 2012. Retrieved
August 1, 2012 (http://money.cnn.com/2012/05/23/
technology/facebook-ipo-what-went-wrong/index.htm).

Schonfeld, Erick. "Tumblr's David Karp: My Heroes Are
Steve Jobs and Willy Wonka." Tech Crunch, February
24, 2011. Retrieved June 21, 2012 (http://techcrunch
.com/2011/02/24/founder-stories-tumblr-karp-jobs
-wonka).

Shontell, Alyson. "All Quiet on the Tumblr Front, But Not
the Back End." *Business Insider*, January 5, 2012.
Retrieved July 1, 2012(http://articles.businessinsider
.com/2012-01-05/tech/30592100_1_tumblr-karp-karp
-investors).

Sohn, Tim. "Tumblr CEO David Karp Discusses the Roots
of Tumblr." *Social Times*, May 29, 2012. Retrieved July

23, 2012 (http://socialtimes.com/tumblr-ceo-david
-karp-discusses-the-roots-of-tumblr_b97221).

Stelter, Brian. "Blogging Site Tumblr Makes Itself the
News." *New York Times*, February 2, 2012. Retrieved
August 2, 2012 (http://www.nytimes.com/2012/02
/02/business/media/tumblr-hires-writers-to-cover
-itself.html).

Technorati. "State of the Blogosphere, 2011." November 4,
2011. Retrieved July 24, 2012 (http://technorati.com
/social-media/article/state-of-the-blogosphere-2011
-introduction).

Thompson, Clive. "The Early Years: A Timeline of the
History of Blogging." *New York Magazine*, February
12, 2006. Retrieved July 19, 2012(http://nymag.com
/news/media/15971).

Ungerleider, Neal. "Tumblr in 2012: More Original
Content." *Fast Company*, January 3, 2012. Retrieved
August 1, 2012 (http://www.fastcompany.com/1805060
/tumblr-2012-more-original-content-less-f-yeah-memes).

Vidyarthi, Neil. "Three Ways Reblogging Is Powering
Tumbler's Growth." *Social Times*, February 2, 2011.
Retrieved July 21, 2012 (http://socialtimes.com/3
-ways-reblogging-is-powering-tumblrs-growth_b36851).

Walker, Rob. "Can Tumblr's David Karp Embrace Ads
Without Selling Out?" *New York Times Magazine*, July
12, 2012. Retrieved July 13, 2012 (http://www
.nytimes.com/2012/07/15/magazine/can-tumblrs

-david-karp-embrace-ads-without-selling-out
.html?pagewanted=all&_moc.semityn.www).

Welch, Liz. "The Way I Work: David Karp of Tumblr."
Inc., June 2011. Retrieved June 30, 2012 (http://www
.inc.com/magazine/201106/the-way-i-work-david
-karp-of-tumblr.html).

Young, Molly. "The Q&A: David Karp, Founder of Tumblr."
More Intelligent Life. Retrieved July 19, 2012 (http://
moreintelligentlife.com/blog/molly-young/qa-david
-karp-founder-tumblr).

Index

ABOUT THE AUTHOR

Monique Vescia is a writer with many nonfiction books, on a variety of subjects, to her credit. The proud owner of a shiny new tumblelog, Monique makes her home in Seattle, Washington, with her husband and fellow writer, Don Rauf, and their son, Leo.

PHOTO CREDITS

Cover, pp. 3, 38–39 Don Emmert/AFP/Getty Images; pp. 6–7 © iStockphoto.com/Thomas Dickson; p. 11 Charley Gallay/WireImage/ Getty Images; p. 14 Charly Kurz/laif/Redux; pp. 16–17 Robert Nickelsberg/Getty Images; pp. 24–25 iStockphoto/Thinkstock; p. 26 © iStockphoto.com/serts; p. 29 Izim M. Gulcuk/Shutterstock.com; p. 31 © iStockphoto.com/Ingvar Bjork; p. 41 John Parra/WireImage/ Getty Images; pp. 42–43 Chester Higgins Jr./The New York Times/ Redux; p. 48 Vallery Jean/FilmMagic/Getty Images; pp. 50–51 Yana Paskova/The New York Times/Redux; p. 54 Bloomberg/ Getty Images; pp. 56–57 © iStockphoto.com/Ismail Akin Bostanci; p. 61 Jason Kempin/WireImage/Getty Images; pp. 64–65 Pixland/ Thinkstock; p. 71 Hiroko Masuike/The New York Times/Redux; pp. 74–75 Bennett Raglin/WireImage/Getty Images; p. 78 Lionsgate/ AP Images; p. 84 Imaginechina/AP Images; pp. 88–89 Charles Eshelman/Getty Images; pp. 92–93 © iStockphoto.com/Andrea Zanchi; pp. 96–97 Toshifumi Kitamura/AFP/Getty Images; p. 101 Nadine Rupp/Getty Images; background image pp. 15, 18, 19, 28, 29, 30, 32, 40, 46, 53, 54, 58, 59, 66, 69, 70, 76, 77, 80, 82, 94, 95, 98, 99 kentoh/Shutterstock.com; cover and remaining interior background image dpaint/Shutterstock.com.

Designer: Brian Garvey; Editor: Nicholas Croce;
Photo Researcher: Karen Huang